The Feedback Loop in Agile

Do work, get feedback and learn, repeat to meet user needs and get value

TJ Rerob

Contents

Chapter One

Intro

Welcome to the feedback loop, and how you can really deliver software value. The concept of feedback on work is not new. The process is tried and true. Though work teams have drifted away from the practice. Especially in teams using more of traditional development practices. Practices that are reliant on driving work thru requirements. Bringing back good feedback to the team will help the team to deliver real value and quality. This eBook will help understand reasons your team stopped using feedback and and benefits of getting back to it.

Why I am qualified for this

Over a 15 year career, entirely in software development team roles, I have observed and experimented with practices for the teams. I have learned what works and what does not work. I continue to leverage these ideas and help grow teams today.

Over the course of my career, I have worked in large Fortune 500 companies, with massive development teams. Those teams working in Agile, working Waterfall, and working something in between. I have also worked in and experienced the start-up culture. As well as other smaller or medium-sized development teams. There are unique challenges on larger and smaller teams, but there are also universal challenges. The concepts I will bring forth will help regardless of team size.

All experience has shaped my ideas. Building them into combinations of ideas and practices that really work. A lot of trial and error has occurred, but it has shaped the information I use today. This information is born of concept and fundamental discussions with many teams and peers.

Intent

This eBook is here to help explain and guide the use of the feedback process on teams. This concept is valuable to any team, but especially so with Agile software development. The concepts and ideas presented will help explain the feedback loop. Help explain reasons and causes that it has been abandoned. I will then reinforce the value of feedback in the Agile team and describe its use in Agile software development.

Always aiming to provide good info and earning your business

In my ebooks I always aim to provide useful, but concise information. I want concepts and ideas to be readily available to be taken and put into practice. I don't aim for over the top elaboration, but try to get to the point. We are all busy, and learning new things shouldn't take hours upon hours. Thus my texts are more concise than some other offerings out there.

Regardless, if you don't feel like you come away with good information or what you expected, I would love to hear about it. Improvement is the name of the game, for myself as well.

Additionally, if I can help to get you to a place where you would consider leaving me a positive review, I would greatly enjoy the chance to do so. I have multiple other offerings already published, and others in the works. Please email me at tj_rerob@outlook.com, if I can help to earn a positive review.

Chapter Two

What is the feedback loop

Feedback loops in Agile are so very important! As that is how you learn and deliver the right things. They are a foundational tool of the Agile process. Over time we have moved away from real feedback. Even attempting to replace feedback loops with other processes. To deliver real quality and value, bring back this learning tool.

Just imagine a process where your Agile team could show work to users. Those users could provide real and honest feedback. Which your team could use to reinforce ideas and to learn. Wouldn't that real feedback be so helpful? That process exists! They are feedback loops in Agile. Which are part of the demo process used on Agile teams.

But what is the feedback loop in Agile? The feedback loop is a more generic term, for the repeating cycle between parties, where information is shared, evaluated, updated, and shared again. Team members can share information, assumptions, and work products with users to get an evaluation. That evaluation is then used to make decisions on how to move forward. The feedback loop applies to so much more than just a demo of software products though. It should also be used to refine information, assumptions, and validations. Refining those through real feedback will only strengthen them. This allows anything you are doing to be made better.

In the following we will further explore feedback. Getting into what it is, reasons we stop using it, benefits to use it and some ways to leverage it. So consider the feedback loop for your team. If not using it, how can you start. If you are using it, how can you leverage it for more learning, and better quality and value?

Chapter Three

Why feedback is so important to the team

The feedback loop is a critical process in learning. Any Agile software development process requires not just trial and error but also learning and adjustment on that learning. Adjusting based on what was learned thru feedback loops. This is especially true in Agile software development teams.

Why feedback loops in Agile?

Much in software development has gone to processes less dependent on feedback. It's believed that the software development team members can research and determine what it is that user needs. While that might be able to be done, it won't always give you the best product. Sometimes it will fail and give you the wrong product. Either way, it will likely take longer than it needs to.

Feedback is a learning process

As I mentioned above, feedback is all about learning. Feedback loops are a do and learn process. The intent is to take deliberate steps in work, that can be evaluated for success. Deliberate and measured steps in the work, that allow for good feedback. Feedback that you can learn from and use to build the next pieces of work.

Ever moving forward, ever evaluating from feedback loops and ever improving.

Feedback facilitates faster results

Build and learn processes allow you to move faster. Results are gained faster because you deliver work, and get feedback on what works and what doesn't. Then you leverage that feedback to fix what doesntdoesnt work. Teams spend less time researching and more time delivering exactly what users need.

Feedback is the best way to know if you meet user needs

There are ways to measure success. In general there are endless data points and metrics that can be used. These can help understand degailsdegails around success more fully. However, the best way to evaluate software products is to go direct to the source. Talk with the actual users and those impacted by the software. Real and honest feedback from those involved will allow the quick learning and course correction that other methods struggle with.

Feedback supports so many of the Agile best practices and values

Feedback supports much of good Agile fundamentals and values for the team. If you look at the 4 Agile values, as presented in the Agile manifesto, they all require feedback. Individuals and interactions over processes and tools. Working software over comprehensive documentation. Customer collaboration over contract negotiation.

Responding to change over following a plan. All of these have an aspect of feedback. Feedback from working with the customer and user. This makes good feedback processes a fundamental aspect of Agile development methodology. More importantly, feedback processes are then fundamental to success of the team.

Chapter Four

Agile and software development processes that need feedback

Let's further consider this idea that Agile fundamental values include and rely on the feedback process. What specific processes utilize and need feedback loops? The following processes and tools need good feedback, in order to be successful.

Shorter iterations

Feedback loops go hand in hand with shorter iterations. The ability to go execute on work in a shorter timeframe, where you show the work to users and get feedback, really depends on that feedback aspect. If you have shorter iterations without getting feedback from users, what is the real delineation of the sprint that makes it a shorter iteration? Simply that some work is maybe deployed to production or made live? Even if that is done without getting feedback, in one form or another, feedback will start to come in from users.

By this, I mean that if you deploy new changes to production without getting good feedback prior, if the changes are not well received, users will start to let you know. That said, of course you don't want to go this route. As a negative reaction can damage your product and your business. Thus use the feedback loop prior. Get feedback from users and test your work before going to production. Use it as a learning process.

Following this path enables the shorter iterations. Your team will build smaller pieces, get feedback, and be able to move forward faster. Learning and shortening the time it takes to refine and deliver what users ultimately need. Which is how the iterations can become shorter.

Improved quality

Quality is improved with good feedback loop processes. This happens by going direct to the source of information. Instead of trying to figure out what users need, you build and get user feedback. This lets you build with quality, right towards user needs. Instead of having to change things to try and get what the user needs.

Teams always strive to build quality. What typically happens that hurts quality is that changes along the way, to meet user needs, force changes to the system to do things that were other than intended. Tweaking logic and architecture, extending beyond how it was originally thought to behave and function. This stems from not having the good feedback needed to build what is needed. By having that feedback built in, the sooner the better, you can reduce those types of tweaks along the way. Ultimately, improving quality.

Iterative and incremental progress forward

Iterative and incremental progress in software development rely on the feedback loop between teams and users. Feedback is the specific trigger at which you determine if you need to continue iterating or adding to the work. The team will keep building new versions and keep expanding on the software in pieces. Feedback is used to determine if something is good enough, or if it is not and needs further work. Both finding if work is good enough, and finding what things are still needed or need to be improved when not good enough, are reliant on a solid feedback process.

Build, learn, repeat

While there are some examples of work where you need to finish the entire thing and you don't have room to iterate over it or have room for failure. There is plenty of work where there is room to build, learn the flaws or fixes needed, go and make changes, and then repeat the process all over. This continuous cycle of doing, learning, and course correcting, will let you move quickly on many work items. It also gets you software products that meet user needs, that meet needs well, and that do it relatively quickly. At least when compared to more traditional requirement gathering processes.

Real evidence and information from users

Getting real information and evidence from users requires feedback processes. You cannot figure out how software products are performing, and if meeting goals, without this info. Whether direct feedback from users, or more indirect feedback via data gathering and analysis, either is real information about the users. You cannot have feedback without these.

Just in Time Requirements

Just in Time Requirements is a process of getting just enough information to be able to work on what is needed. Enough information to move forward. Or enough information to do some work and enable the feedback process. That is another way of looking at Just in Time Reqs. Its a process of getting enough to do enough work, to get to the next round of feedback processes.

Just in Time Reqs is never about finding out all of the information. It admits that you really can't anyways. Not without missing something or doing something incorrectly. So its much better to attempt the work in manageable pieces. Do small pieces of work and then evaluate it to see if it meets user needs. Learn from it and then build onto it. Thats where its part in the feedback process comes in.

Testing assumptions requires feedback

There is no real way to verify if your assumptions are correct, other than some sort of real feedback. This could be actual user feedback. That is the most useful. It could also be indirect feedback from observing the actions of users and collecting data on their interactions with your assumptions. If actual user feedback is not available, that is the next best thing. Good feedback loops is maybe the best single way to deliver quality software.

Get info, determine solutions, get feedback, repeat

The process for getting feedback can be simple, if you let it be. We often over crowd the process with formalized rules and frameworks, and that gets in the way. But what you need is simple. You need feedback from actual users. Do you best work, and do that in smaller increments. Then get it in front of users as fast as possible.

Get their feedback and learn from it. Then adjust your work and repeat the process all over again. We let so many things interfere with this. But for truly great quality and products, not to mention to do them in smaller timeframes, feedback loops are absolutely critical. Improve your software quality by getting quick feedback from users.

The scientific process uses feedback by testing a created hypothesis

The scientific process is all about getting feedback, from testing a created hypothesis. Scientists use feedback to test their problems. It's the way they get the most accurate solutions to their problems. They research and hypothesize. Then create solutions and test them. Measuring the results of the testing. That measurement of test results is a feedback process. It is different in that often their process is not interacting with users of something. However, for the process and end result, that really makes no difference. In software, if you are trying to solve a users problem or meet a users goal, the only real way to know if you did is by getting feedback from the user. They are the single best source of information.

Feedback loops in Agile – Include in your processes

I believe the single best way to improve software is by using feed-back loops. Embrace the feedback aspect of your Agile development process. Don't bypass the interactions with users and stakeholders. Remember the ideas of the Agile manifesto, especially around individuals and interactions over processes and tools. Build your work around those interactions to really unlock efficiency, quality and value. The interactions with users and stakeholders will enable help you reach the goals of your Agile project.

Chapter Five

The fundamentals of good feedback

What are fundamental practices that make up good feedback? The below explores some of these ideas. Use them to build up your feedback processes. This will only further enable your team to get the info it needs, to ultimately build the things it needs and meet goals.

Open and honest communication

Be honest with criticism. Be professional. Don't be overly negative, but don't hide items that missed the mark either. Promote that honesty with the users. You need to have real and honest communication to get to the needs of the user and stakeholder. Avoiding issues only prolongs fixing of said issues.

Direct communication

This goes along with being honest, but be direct with the communication. Beating around the bush hides the details. Going around or hiding the information needed, will only stop items from being addressed. You have to be direct, to be able to really communicate. If you can do this, and promote tackling of the issues head on, you will really ramp up your feedback processes.

Real evaluation of needs

Expanding on honesty and direct communication, you need to have conversations about the needs of the users and stakeholders. Really dive into the details of their needs. This conversation will build team understanding of the needs, and most importantly, enable them to figure out how to meet said needs. If needs are not discussed and communicated, feedback processes don't work.

Be ready to learn and go again

Remember its a process of iterative development. You build, learn, and refine. You can't always get it right on the first attempt. Honestly, you will often not get it right on the first attempt, and probably attempts after that. But you will make progress towards where you need to be. The feedback processes are an opportunity to learn what works, what doesn't, and then make changes. You course correct, to keep making progress towards the goals. You have to remember that part, that its a learn and adapt process. So keep that good feedback, so that you can learn and adapt.

Chapter Six

Reasons we moved away from feedback loops

Feedback processes have dropped off. A lot of this is because of the importance of requirements in the software development process. This is not the only reason though. Here are some reasons why good feedback loops took a hit. Work on these and bring back better feedback to your Agile processes.

Why we strayed from getting feedback

It is my opinion that as processes evolved and improved, we sought ways to bypass feedback. Maybe this was thought of as an efficiency gain. Where it was using up too much time of users, to get the feedback. Thus a better process would be where we could figure out the information without the users and keep moving forward. That is just not the case.

Maybe it was thought that as a natural progression of learning for team members, they will grow and do not need to get as much user feedback. This is also not the case. As they learn software, products, the business needs, it only means they might not need as much information to get started. It does not change the requirement for feedback. The feedback loop is still critical. Not getting feedback soon enough in the process is a primary issue with Waterfall development methodology.

Requirements sought as a way to replace feedback

Another reason I think we strayed is because of more traditional software development methods, involving requirements. Requirements are meant to tell the team exactly what is needed. They are a list of needs and goals that drive the work of the team. Often they are created as part of a formal and structured process, involving business users. The business users sign off on the requirements and the team executes on them. However, the requirements don't tell the full story. Also, without something visual and tangible items for users to evaluate, they might not know all of the requirements. Making it impossible to be able to provide them. Nonetheless, we created the requirement process to try and get all information determined upfront, to go do the work.

Trying to get all of the requirements up front also comes from project management techniques and processes. In that, for software projects, the requirements are attempted to be figured out prior. So that you can organize resources around the work. Then you can organize time and budget to those resources. A major flaw in this is that you just can't understand all of the requirements up front. The waterfall model is at a disadvantage against Agile methods when you are dealing with complex and changing requirements. You simply can't understand all of the details around requirements up front, let alone know the time and effort it will take to complete them.

We try to figure it out prior

Often we think we can figure it all out ourselves. Instead, we should figure out enough to start. Then get pieces of work ready enough for feedback. A trend in software and product work is to try and do an upfront understanding of the work. I argue there is a big difference between planning around doing work, and trying to figure out the work ahead of time. It's ok to plan for work, to try and figure out things your team may need to tackle the work. On the other hand, trying to figure out the details of that work well before doing the work causes issues. Trying to figure out the details of the work is not part of the Agile scrum development methodology.

Expectations influence completion

A popular theme in software development is the due date of the work. A due date is determined before the work, by those not doing the work. This is supposed to be when the work should be done. However, the work should be done when the software or product meets a needed goal, not an arbitrary date. Shift expectations, from expecting a finished work product because a date is reached. Allow iterations to be times of inspection of the work, to alter course and see if the work is done. If it is, great. If it is not, the work continues. You have to allow for growth, to leverage the feedback loop. This is part of an iterative mindset and good Agile process.

Embrace the criticism, but use it only to move forward

Along the way, we struggled with the criticism. But we shouldn't be afraid of it, we should learn from it. Criticism is the backbone of the feedback loop. It depends on real and constructive criticism. Some cultures hold it against the team members if feedback dictates that they greatly change their work. Or in other words, they were wrong and need to make changes and fixes. I argue that first, that is part of the process and will happen at times. Second, you could not get to that feedback and make adjustments, if it had not been for the first work and the ability to get real feedback. So use it, and learn from it. Criticism comes from interaction with users and stakeholders, and it is useful to the team. So use it to help improve software quality, your efficiency and deliver business value.

As product owner, scrummaster, or even project manager, enable the feedback loops for the team. Don't interfere with or hamper that feedback. The team needs it to succeed. Especially in an Agile environment.

Get back to better solutions thru the feedback loop
Here are some ways we can get back to better solutions by using the feedback loop. These ideas will help promote good feedback which increases the your product and software quality.

Chapter Seven

Requirements took over instead of good feedback

Expanding further on requirements, but diving into why they can't be the only part of your process. There is room for requirements in your Agile development, however they can't be the only way to get the info to build towards your goals.

Requirements Are Too Stringent Of A Guideline

Requirements are a definition to be followed. They are stringent guidelines of the work to be done. This can lead to a lack of creativity or a lack of innovation. The feeling is that the requirement is dictating the work and that is what must be done. This stifles the team's ability to build the best solution they can.

The rigidity of requirements is something that goes against agile methodologies. In agile, responding to change is a guiding thought. Following requirements strictly, and responding to change, are at odds with each other. This inflexibility is a drawback with requirements. But, what's better than requirements?

Before getting into that, I first have to go out on a limb. I would argue that requirements should not exist in agile software development. The information is needed, but the concept of a requirement is too stringent. What's better than requirements? There are processes available that don't follow strict requirements. They use goals, or actual user feedback to determine the work.

Feedback loops in Agile win over requirements in any example

I just completed working from an extensive and detailed list of requirements. The team had delivered a quality product. More so than that, they had put a lot of time and effort into this work. Then, the product was delivered Immediately, the users said, "well, what about this....". We were a bit dejected, to say the least! We had worked from the requirements and thought we delivered what was needed. Just to find out the hard way, maybe there is something better to use than requirements.

In software development, requirements are often the driving factor of the output. They are treated as the end-all and be all. They are what the team is trying to deliver. Requirements are used to tell the team what it is that they have to deliver. Often they are a stringent list of details. To guide the team to the final product. However, they are often incomplete.

Requirements are often incomplete

Could there be a better way? A way to guide work without telling the team exactly what to do. Could requirements not be all they are cracked up to be? What's better than requirements? In the following, I discuss some drawbacks of requirements. Common problems with requirements. Issues from traditional requirement driven processes. I then discuss some alternative approaches. Ways that align with agile and help the team deliver.

What's Better Than Requirements – Feedback Loops in Agile

- Working towards goals
- Understanding needs
- Getting honest, timely feedback

Working towards goals gives the team the ability to see the endgame and visualize a path to get there. By understanding where they need to get to, the team is better able to build towards that goal. The team can create solutions with goals in mind, thus getting better solutions. Understand goals, and fill in with information to support the delivery on said goals. Use the goals to guide the work. They are high-level details, almost like high-level requirements. Fill in the details as you do the work. This lets you achieve more, and deliver a better product.

Use goals as high level details to guide the work. Then fill in the details as you work it, for a better product.

Understanding needs has the same effect. It allows the team to build towards a goal, but to do so in a way that helps the user. There are lots of options for getting to a goal, but finding something that the user benefits from is understanding their needs. This is why goals and needs are whats better than requirements.

Getting honest and timeline feedback is how you fine-tune the work being done. Build fast, fail fast, and learn fast, so that you can course correct. You will never know everything. Instead, get useable pieces in front of those who will use it. Then get their feedback. This lets you figure out how to fix what you have. Also, how to add what you still need. Ultimately moving towards the goal of the finished product. This is why real feedback is what's better than requirements.

When Are You Done

With requirements, sometimes you don't know when you are done. Conventional wisdom states if you complete the requirements that you have completed the work. However, without knowing the goal you are trying to achieve, you don't necessarily know if you are done. The team is strictly following a path laid out before work started. It is unclear from the requirements alone if goals were met. It is not always certain if requirements are still valid while the work is going on.

With requirements, the team can be lulled into a false sense of security, in that requirements are exactly what is needed. Surprise, sometimes they are wrong! Like anything, requirements have an element of error in them. Working off them strictly can lead down the wrong path. Requirements can be based on faulty assumptions and information. Strictly following them leads to errors.

Final Thoughts On Whats Better Than Requirements

Ultimately, whats better than requirements is a mindset that problem solves. A mindset that is flexible and adaptable. This is an agile mindset. Requirements are all about defining the work to be done prior. Knowing what is needed. Also knowing the tools to be used, processes, and how to go do the work. In the real world, this is not feasible. You have new work that is full of unknowns. There are changing needs and technology landscapes. These things don't allow the team to know everything before they start the work. The way to approach is to work towards needs and goals, figuring out the best way forward at each piece of work. Also, getting good feedback from users and stakeholders. This is an agile mindset and approach. What's better than requirements, is ultimately an agile approach to the work.

Chapter Eight

How to bring it back to the team

Remember your Agile principles and values! The interactions of individuals is more important than any process or tool. Feedback is gained from individuals having those interactions. Especially when those interactions are between the team and the users.

Working software is more important than documentation. A huge reason for this is that it shows the users what it is doing and what it can do. By getting working software out there, the team can use it to get more feedback from users. Ultimately refining their work and best meeting user needs. This is way easier and faster than trying to discuss without having working software to show. Or way easier than presenting documentation.

Chapter Nine

Feedback processes

Here are a few of the processes in software development that rely on good feedback processes.

Demo

This is one of the biggest. It is so critical to have good feedback from the demo of software. Otherwise, what is the point? If showing software to users and stakeholders to get feedback, and you don't get feedback or you get feedback that doesn't help, there really is no point in the demo. You absolutely need good feedback, as part of a demo, to be effective.

User surveys

Surveys are a great way to sample opinions and information at the leisure of the user. Users that respond to surveys will often provide great insight into the things that they don't like about software and products. 2 large drawbacks here are that you might not have the right sampling to determine if an issue provided by some users is an issue for a large enough subset of your user base. Large enough to take on work to resolve. Another issue is that it can be tough to get some users to respond to surveys. Again making it difficult to get feedback from a good representation of your user base. All in all, they are an effective tool, but should be used in conjunction with outher methods.

Monitoring

Monitoring users as they use products. This is a great one to get feedback without the influence of others on the user's opinion. Essentially, you monitor users, but in such a way as they don't really feel your monitoring. You can see how they really use software and pick up on tendencies and issues that maybe even the user isn't aware of.

Data and analytics

A great tool to see trends and issues at scale in your software products. By collecting data, often through web based analytics but not always so, you can see bigger picture uses cases and items with your products. Things a user in direct feedback might not represent.

User acceptance tests and test environments for users

A last item is the user acceptance tests and/or having test environments for users. These are valuable to help get software products to the final stages or to refine software products. User acceptance is typically when you are trying to complete some work. You get the users to give their ok. It is a form of feedback from the user. Same with the test environment, if you set it up in such a way that users outside of the team can access and use.

Chapter Ten

Benefits of feedback loop processes

And for the benefits of feedback in Agile software development. The below items are to be gained by using good feedback. Having feedback in your development processes.

Why feedback loops in Agile are important

Feedback lets you know if on the right track

Feedback will let you know if you are on the right track. Which in turn will allow for course corrections to continue to better the software or product. Or to fix issues entirely. You would not know if you are on the wrong track if you don't get honest and timely feedback.

Feedback avoids builder bias

Feedback from users will not contain the bias of the person that created something. Often, the creator of something can miss things. Because they make assumptions to steer their creation. Those assumptions can cause things to be overlooked. Actual users only care about using the product according to their needs. If you can get feedback from them, they will provide that feedback accordingly.

Feedback enables building of the right things

Feedback processes help you to select and build the right things. The right work to meet the needs and goals of your user and organization. Not just being on the right. But also picking the right things to do next.

Less waste

Feedback enables you to have less wasted work. It does this in 2 main ways. First, you go down the right path and build the right things. Because feedback helps hone the goals and narrow the focus, you do the right work that your company needs. The second way is that by getting good feedback, you know when you are done. Once you meet needs and goals, you can move onto the next set of work. Avoiding a scenario where you keep working on something, adding additional work that isn't necessary.

Enables faster more efficient building

By getting feedback more often, you course correct and avoid the wrong work. This makes for a faster and more efficient process. Ultimately, you will meet your goals faster when you use good feedback processes.

Get the details you can't get other ways

Feedback processes enable you to get the details you can't get without user collaboration. IE, collecting requirements, or expert input on what and how to build things, and more. All can lead to misses. Often they have misses in some way or another. What varies is the severity of the misses. Using feedback embraces that you will have misses, and fixes them.

Chapter Eleven

Contact

As always, I like to continue learning and further my ideas. Drop me a line if you would like to discuss further.

Find more @ Agile Rant

TJ Rerob is a founder and top contributor at Agile Rant. Agile Rant is an online publication on Agile, software development, product, teamwork, leadership and other modern practices. Blog postings explore questions and issues and dive into items to help explore and find answers.

https://www.agilerant.info

Please sign up for the Agile Rant newsletter

@ https://www.agilerant.info/connect-with-agile-rant/.
There you will gain access to deals on books, notices on upcoming content, access to the existing library of content, and more. Your email will never be sold or spammed. This is for readers interested in more Agile Rant content.

Lastly, feel free to connect via our social media accounts:

https://www.instagram.com/agile_rant
https://www.twitter.com/AgileRant
https://www.facebook.com/Agile.Rant1.0/

Upcoming content

Guide for Vertical Slicing of User Stories
Always posting new blog entires and helpful content at https://www.agilerant.info/